Pronunciation Poems

PronPack 4
Pronunciation Poems

- A four-book set for teachers of English
- Fun-packed pronunciation activities
- Easy-to-follow presentation notes
- Extra resources on PronPack.com
- Print-friendly worksheets

By Mark Hancock

Hancock McDonald
ENGLISH LANGUAGE TEACHING

PronPack 4
Pronunciation Poems
By Mark Hancock

ENGLISH LANGUAGE TEACHING

Published by **Hancock McDonald ELT**
Chester. CH1 2AW UK
www.hancockmcdonald.com

First Published 2017

ISBN: 978-0-9957575-4-7

Contents

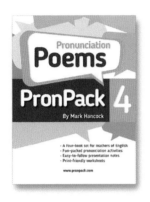

End Matter

Introduction

The Book

What is PronPack?

PronPack is a set of four resource books to help teachers focus on English pronunciation in class. The books contain printable worksheets along with teacher's notes explaining how to use them. Each of the four books takes a slightly different approach to pronunciation teaching. You can select the approach you prefer, or use the various books to complement one another.

What are Pronunciation Poems?

Pronunciation Poems are rhymes, chants, limericks, raps and song lyrics all written specifically to contain multiple examples of the target pronunciation features. The activities usually begin with an exercise completing or correcting the text and culminate in practising saying or chanting the text out loud.

What are the benefits of doing these poems?

The poems can benefit learners by making specific features of English pronunciation very noticeable to them because they occur so frequently in a short sample of language. They also provide concentrated practice in producing the target feature through the chant. A further benefit is that they tend to be very memorable – the chant or lyric will often 'play-on-repeat' in the student's head afterwards, providing extra silent practice.

What aspects of pronunciation are covered in PronPack 4?

The poems in the greater part of the book focus on individual sounds. Later in the book there are poems focusing on consonant clusters, grammatical *–ed* and *–s* endings and weak forms. However, the poems all have a further focus which is equally if not more important: they provide intensive exemplification and practice of connected speech.

What are the other books in the PronPack collection?

The other books in the series are:

PronPack 1: Pronunciation Workouts – extended choral drill activities.

PronPack 2: Pronunciation Puzzles – puzzles and game-like activities.

PronPack 3: Pronunciation Pairworks – communication activities.

The Approach

Why teach pronunciation?

The most important reason to teach pronunciation is to help your students understand and be understood. As listeners, they need to learn how other speakers blend sounds into words and words into connected speech. As speakers, they need to modify their own accent of English to make it as widely intelligible as possible. Neither of these objectives requires them to precisely copy the accent of a native speaker. The aim is successful communication, not 'correctness'.

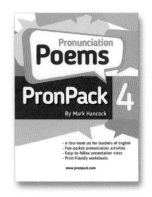

What is the pronunciation model?

In the context of your classroom, the best pronunciation model is almost certainly you, the teacher. PronPack aims to be as flexible as possible - you should be able to work with it whether your own accent is from London or Sydney, Turkey or Argentina. Although the phonemic symbols used are based on a British model, they are not intended to be prescriptive. For instance, /e/ does not specify the precise quality of the vowel, but merely that it is different from /æ/ or /ɪ/.

Do I have to know the phonemic alphabet?

You don't have to know or use the phonemic alphabet for the poems. Phonemic symbols are sometimes used as headings in parts of the activity, but the activity does not depend on the student knowing them.

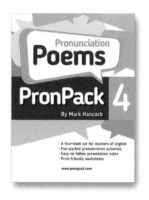

Do these activities work only for one accent?

The poems do not restrict you to teaching towards a specific accent – they should work for a variety of accents, including American. However, the audio files, if you choose to use them, are recorded in a General British accent. Note that there is both a British and an American English version of the **PronPack Sound Chart**.

Note that the symbols which appear between slanted brackets in this book, such as /ʌ/ or /ʃ/, are strictly speaking, phonemes rather than sounds. A phoneme such as /ʌ/ corresponds to slightly different sounds across different accents.

Flexi notes throughout the books highlight ways that you can adapt the material to work with different accents.

The Activities

What materials are in the book?

The book contains printable worksheets for the students and teacher's notes for you. The teacher's notes highlight the teaching focus, minimum level, and indicate printing requirements and audio files for each activity. The notes give a short background to the pronunciation point plus step-by-step activities for using the activity in class.

How long do the activities take?

Each activity will typically take around 15-20 minutes of class time, although this can vary a lot depending on how thoroughly you exploit the material. If you would like to spend longer, you can combine the *poem* with a *workout*, *puzzle* or *pairwork* activity focusing on the same pronunciation point from **PronPack 1**, **2** and **3**. Recommended combinations are given in the *Lesson Plans* section, page 10 and in the **Goes well with ...** notes at the end of each activity.

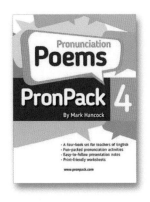

Do I have to print out the worksheets?

The worksheets in **Pronunciation Poems** can be printed out, or alternatively, you could project them. However, for many of the activities, it is better if the student have their printed copy so they can write in any corrections or fill any gaps.

What level are the activities designed for?

The minimum level is indicated in the teacher's notes for each poem, but remember that this is a minimum level. An activity which is suitable for a pre-intermediate learner can be just as valuable for an upper intermediate learner – pronunciation often lags behind other competences because it has been neglected.

Are the activities for a specific age group or class size?

The activities are not aimed at a specific age group and can benefit young learners and adults alike. On the other hand, there may be some adults, both teachers and students, who don't feel that chants, raps and songs are appropriate, so you will need to use your own judgement here. However, all the poems have been trialled in adult classes and have worked well. The poems in this book will function in any size of class.

What are the audio files for?

There are audio files for all of the poems. These always include a version of the text read out in plain speech. In many cases, however, there is a second version, which is the text set to a backing track to make it into a rap, chant or song. In some cases, there is also an audio file of just the backing track, without the words, so that the students can chant over it.

However, you can choose not to use the audio at all and simply model the texts in your own voice, and this works perfectly well. If you do this, it is wise to practise saying the poem a couple of times before class so that you know where difficulties might lie for your students.

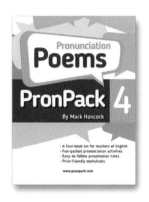

The Website

What will I find on the support website?

PronPack.com provides additional information for users of **PronPack** including downloadable poster versions of the *PronPack Sound Charts* and Free extra pronunciation activities.

If you have purchased an ePub or the print-version of this book we would like to thank you for supporting our endeavour. On the website you will have access to teacher resources to accompany the activities including:

- Print-friendly PDF files of the activity worksheets

- Slides to use during the presentation phase of the lessons

- Downloadable MP3 audio files as required

- Updates and additional materials

Note: The interactive functionality of the fixed-layout ePub will depend on your device and/or the ePub reader available for your device.

Contact us

We'd welcome your feedback on www.pronpack.com and invite you to share your thoughts and reactions on the book seller's website.

Please get in touch with us through our website if you have any difficulties with the material or would like to make a suggestion for another activity.

Connect with us on:

 twitter.com/pronpackbooks (@pronpackbooks)

 facebook.com/pronpack

Lesson Plans

If you plan to focus on a particular pronunciation point, here are some recommended activity combinations from across the **PronPack Collection** (books **1**, **2**, **3** and **4**):

- Awareness of sounds: **2.1** and **2.6**

- The complete sound system: **1.1**, **1.2** and **1.3**

- Long versus short vowels: **3.1** Version 1, **3.2** Version 2 and **4.1**

- The *R* vowels: **1.4**, **2.2** Version 4 and **4.3**

- Vowels spelt with 2 letters: **1.5**, **2.12**, **2.2** Version 5 and **4.4**

- Short vowels: **1.6**, **2.3**, **3.1** Version 2, **3.3** vowel pairs and **4.2**

- Stop consonants: **1.7**, **3.4** Version 1, **3.3** consonant pairs and **4.11**

- Fricatives and affricates: **1.8**, **2.2** Version 2, **3.4** Version 3, **4.9** and **4.10**

- Semi-vowels: **2.2** Version 3, **3.4** Version 2 and **4.7**

- /l/ versus /r/: **3.2** Version 3, **3.5** Version 3 and **4.8**

- Consonant clusters: **1.9** and **4.13**

- *-ed* endings: **2.2** Version 6 and **4.14**

- /s/ versus /z/ and *–s* endings: **2.2** Version 1, **3.5** Version 2 and **4.15**

- Word stress: **2.9** and **3.6**

- Word stress families: **1.10**, **2.7**, **3.8** and **4.16**

- Weak forms: **1.11**, **2.4** Version 2, **4.5** and **4.17**

- Rhythm: **1.12** and **4.16**

- Tonic stress: **1.13**, **2.9**, **3.10**, **3.11** and **3.12**

- Connected speech: **2.5**, **2.10**, and **3.9**

Goes well with ...

... These combinations are also given at the end of each activity.

Map of the Book

The PronPack Sound Chart	A teaching and reference tool for the individual sounds of English, including an explanatory Infographic. This book has two versions of the Chart: **IPA** with guidewords and **American** with guidewords.		
POEMS	**TEACHING FOCUS**	**MINIMUM LEVEL**	**ACTIVITY**
4.1 **Get up on your Feet**	The vowels /iː/ and /ɪ/	Pre-intermediate	Chanting or reciting
4.2 **In the Woods**	The short vowels: /ɪ, e, æ, ʌ, ʊ, ə, ɒ/	Intermediate	Chanting or reciting
4.3 **That Girl**	The vowels which precede the letter *r* : /eə, ɑː, ɜː, ɔː, ɪə, ə/	Pre-intermediate	Reciting or singing
4.4 **Cat and Mouse**	The vowels spelt with the digraph *ou*: /aʊ, uː, ɒ, ʌ, ɔː, ə/	Pre-intermediate	Chanting or reciting
4.5 **Schwa Limericks**	The schwa phoneme /ə/	Pre-intermediate	Chanting or reciting
4.6 **Hannah's Horse**	The consonant /h/	Pre-intermediate	Chanting or reciting
4.7 **One Windy Wednesday**	The consonant /w/	Pre-intermediate	Chanting or reciting
4.8 **Luck**	The consonants /r/ and /l/	Pre-intermediate	Reciting or singing
4.9 **A Footballer's Story**	The consonants /dʒ/ and /tʃ/	Intermediate	Chanting or reciting
4.10 **Sue's Shoes**	The consonants /s/ and /ʃ/	Pre-intermediate	Chanting or reciting
4.11 **Flatmates**	The voiced consonants /b, d, g, v, z/ in word-final position	Intermediate	Chanting or reciting
4.12 **Kittens and Buttons**	The glottal stop sound ʔ	Intermediate	Chanting or reciting
4.13 **Steve on Skis**	Initial consonant clusters	Intermediate	Chanting or reciting
4.14 **Lost**	The pronunciation of *–ed* endings	Pre-intermediate	Chanting or reciting
4.15 **Bananas**	The pronunciation of *-s* endings	Pre-intermediate	Chanting or reciting
4.16 **Further Education**	Stress patterns in longer words	Intermediate	Chanting or reciting
4.17 **Vicky and Ricky**	The weak forms of pronouns *he, she, her, his, him, it, they, their, them*	Pre-intermediate	Chanting or reciting
4.18 **Nobody does it Better**	Rhythm and weak forms	Pre-intermediate	Chanting or reciting

The PronPack Sound Chart

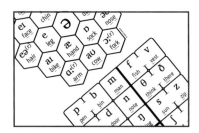

What is the Sound Chart for?

Reference

The **PronPack Sound Chart** is primarily a reference tool. Teachers may print a copy as large as possible to put on the classroom wall. Whenever a pronunciation point comes up in class relating to one or more of the individual sounds, you can point it out on the chart.

Over time, the class will become more and more familiar with it. However, to get students started with the chart, you may want to devote some class time to presenting and exploring it more intensively. There are lessons focusing on the chart in **PronPack 1: Pronunciation Workouts**.

Orientation

The **PronPack Sound Chart** is intended to help you and the class find your way around the sounds of English. It enables you to see the 'big picture' – the entire system – at a glance. This is useful because if you just encounter the sounds one by one, you have no idea of where you are in the system as a whole. It could appear limitless and consequently impossible to master.

Comparison

The **PronPack Sound Chart** graphically represents relationships between the sounds, showing those that are comparable with each other and those which are very different. This helps to promote an understanding of the whole system, as well as making it more memorable. Regular users will eventually be able to remember which sound occupies which place in the chart as a whole.

How is the Sound Chart organised?

The **PronPack Sound Chart Infogaphic** on page 15 explains how the Sound Chart is organised. This is primarily for you, but you could print it out for your students at the beginning of the course too.

Note: You will find downloadable poster versions of the **PronPack Sound Charts** at www.pronpack.com

Chart 1 IPA Phonemic Symbols with Guide Words

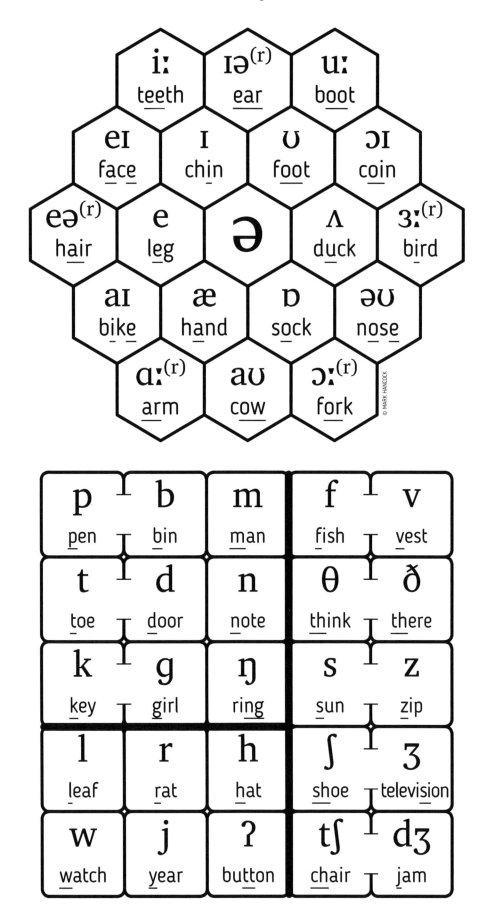

i: teeth | ɪə(r) ear | u: boot

eɪ face | ɪ chin | ʊ foot | ɔɪ coin

eə(r) hair | e leg | ə | ʌ duck | ɜː(r) bird

aɪ bike | æ hand | ɒ sock | əʊ nose

ɑː(r) arm | aʊ cow | ɔː(r) fork

© MARK HANCOCK

p pen	b bin	m man	f fish	v vest
t toe	d door	n note	θ think	ð there
k key	g girl	ŋ ring	s sun	z zip
l leaf	r rat	h hat	ʃ shoe	ʒ television
w watch	j year	ʔ button	tʃ chair	dʒ jam

Chart 2 American Symbols with Guide Words

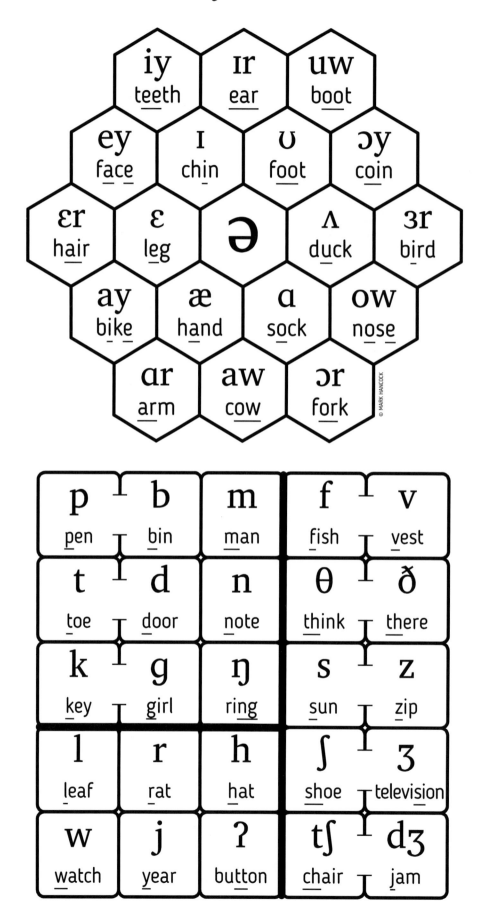

Vowels
in the hexagon...

Six Long vowels
Symbols usually have : but /eə/ also considered a long vowel in this model.

Corners

Outer Circle

Six Diphthongs
Symbols have two elements; the sound moves from one position to the other.

Sides

Six Short vowels
Symbols are all single; these vowels never end a syllable.

Inner Circle

Jaw and lip positions

closed, wide — closed, round
mid - wide — relaxed
open, wide — open, round

The weak vowel
Also known as 'schwa'; only used in unstressed syllables; the most common sound in English!

ə

Centre

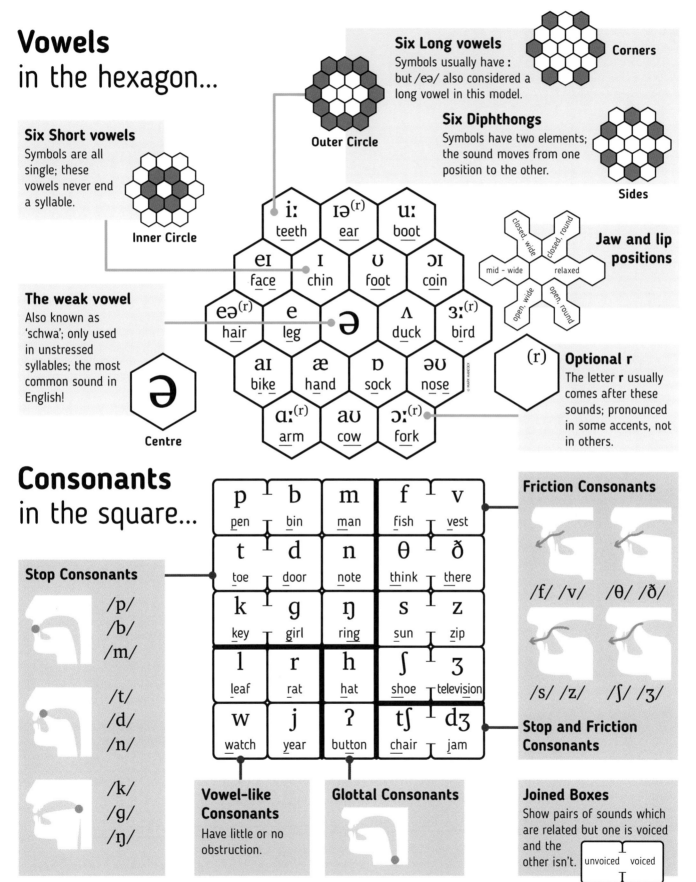

i: teeth
ɪə(r) ear
u: boot
eɪ face
ɪ chin
ʊ foot
ɔɪ coin
eə(r) hair
e leg
ə
ʌ duck
ɜː(r) bird
aɪ bike
æ hand
ɒ sock
əʊ nose
ɑː(r) arm
aʊ cow
ɔː(r) fork

© MARK HANCOCK

(r) **Optional r**
The letter **r** usually comes after these sounds; pronounced in some accents, not in others.

Consonants
in the square...

Stop Consonants

/p/
/b/
/m/

/t/
/d/
/n/

/k/
/g/
/ŋ/

p pen	b bin	m man	f fish	v vest
t toe	d door	n note	θ think	ð there
k key	g girl	ŋ ring	s sun	z zip
l leaf	r rat	h hat	ʃ shoe	ʒ television
w watch	j year	ʔ button	tʃ chair	dʒ jam

Friction Consonants

/f/ /v/   /θ/ /ð/

/s/ /z/   /ʃ/ /ʒ/

Stop and Friction Consonants

Vowel-like Consonants
Have little or no obstruction.

Glottal Consonants

Joined Boxes
Show pairs of sounds which are related but one is voiced and the other isn't. unvoiced voiced

Get up on your Feet

Gotta **move** a little (**bit/beat**)
Kick your **feet** to the (**bit/beat**)
(Fill/Feel) the **heat**, that's **it**!

TEACHING FOCUS

To familiarize students with the vowels /iː/ and /ɪ/

MINIMUM LEVEL

Pre-intermediate

ACTIVITY

Chanting or reciting

WORKSHEETS

PronPack Worksheet 4.1
Print one copy for each student

AUDIO FILES

Background

This activity is based on a poem containing a number of minimal pairs of the vowels /iː/ and /ɪ/. The minimal pairs are: **feet** and **fit**, **seat** and **sit**, **feel** and **fill**, **beat** and **bit**, **heat** and **hit**.

Presentation

Write the phrase **keep fit** on the board. Ask students to say what activities they do to keep fit.

Activity

1. Give out the *Worksheet 4.1*. Explain that the text is a short poem and that the last word in alternate lines rhyme. Ask students to look at the words in brackets, choose the one which makes more sense in the context, and underline it.

2. Read out the poem, **Get up on your Feet** (below, with corrections), or play *Audio 4.1-1* (poem sung as a rap 4 times) and ask students to check their answers. They may not be able to do this from listening alone, however, so check the **answers** together as a class afterwards.

   > Get up on your feet
   > *You won't get **fit***
   > *Just sitting on a **seat***
   > *If you wanna get **fit***
   > *Gotta get up on your **feet***
   >
   > *Don't fill that **seat***
   > *Gotta move a little **bit***
   > *Kick your feet to the **beat***
   > ***Feel** the heat, that's it!*

3. Explain that the pairs of words in brackets sound similar, but the first has a short vowel sound and the second has a long vowel sound. For the first sound, the muscles are more relaxed while for the second, the muscles tense and the lips are spread as if smiling.

4. Say some of the words in brackets at random and ask students to say if you are saying the first or the second word.

5. Get students to work in pairs and take turns to speak and listen. One says one of the words in brackets and the other says if it is the first or the second word.

6. Say the poem, leaving a space after each two lines for students to repeat them, or use *Audio 4.1-2*. Point out that the words in bold in the poem show where the stress/beat falls.

7. Ask the class to say the poem together. You may use *Audio 4.1-3* to give them a rhythm to sing over.

Goes well with ...

... **PronPack 3.1** Version 1 and **3.2** Version 2 for a lesson on long versus short vowels.

4.1 Get up on your Feet

Look at the words in brackets. Underline the better of the two.

You **won't** get (**fit/feet**)
Just **sit**ting on a (**sit/seat**)
If you **wan**na get (**fit/feet**)
Gotta **get** up on your (**fit/feet**)

Don't **fill** that (**sit/seat**)
Gotta **move** a little (**bit/beat**)
Kick your **feet** to the (**bit/beat**)
(**Fill/Feel**) the **heat**, that's **it**!

In the Woods

Big Jack and Little Zack
Lived up in the woods

TEACHING FOCUS

To familiarize students with the short vowels: /ɪ, e, æ, ʌ, ʊ, ɒ, ə/

MINIMUM LEVEL

Pre-intermediate

ACTIVITY

Chanting or reciting

WORKSHEETS

PronPack Worksheet 4.2
Print one copy for each student

AUDIO FILES

Background

This activity is based on a poem in which all of the words contain one of the following short vowel sounds: /ɪ, e, æ, ʌ, ʊ, ɒ, ə/.

Flexi: You can modify *Worksheet 4.2* for American symbols. Cross out the /e/ and replace it with /ɛ/ (different symbol, but it represents the same sound). Cross out the /ɒ/ and replace it with /ɑ/ (different sound - /ɒ/ does not exist in American English).

Activity

1. Give out the *Worksheet 4.2*. Tell students to fold it along the dotted line and look only at the top half. Tell them to look at the words outside of the hexagon shapes and check the vocabulary. Ask students to match them with the words inside the hexagons according to the vowel sounds. Check answers: **1.** big – **lived**; **2.** wolf – **good**; **3.** dead – **went**; **4.** and – **as**; **5.** hunt – **son**; **6.** axe – **track**; **7.** chop – **shot**

   Note: the word **as** can be pronounced with the same vowel sound as **axe** when it is said on its own, but the vowel is reduced to a schwa when it is pronounced in context.

2. Explain that all of the words in the exercise that the students have just done come from a story. Ask students to work in pairs and suggest what the story is about. Help them with the meanings of any unknown words.

3. Say the poem, **In the Woods** (below) or play *Audio 4.2-1* (a rap of the poem in this activity, with the final 3 lines repeated once). Tell students to listen and check their ideas from **Step 2**.

   In the Woods
   Big Jack and little Zack
   Lived up in the woods
   Jack was good at hunting
   And Zack, at chopping wood

Jack got up
And had a cup
And went off with his gun
Had some luck
And shot a duck
And cooked it for his son

That son of Jack's
Took an axe
And went off up the track
Cut some wood
Said that's good
And put it on his back

As Zack packed
A wolf attacked
It jumped on that lad's head
That's when Jack
Ran up the track
And shot that big dog dead

DIAGRAM 4.2A

4. Tell students to unfold the page and look at the poem. Say the poem again or play *Audio 4.2-1* and let them listen and read.

5. Tell students to write the following words from the song in **Hexagon 4**: *the, was, at, a, some, for, an, as*. Explain that these all have the same vowel sound in the context of normal fast speech.

   Explain that all of the other words in the song contain one of the other six vowels. Ask them to find at least two examples for each of the vowel sounds.

6. Check the answers together (**DIAGRAM 4.2A**) and get the students to say the words, paying attention to the vowel sound.

7. Say the poem again or play *Audio 4.2-1* and ask students to join in. They repeat this step a few times until they are able to do it fluently.

Flexi: The symbols used on this worksheet are not intended to be prescriptive. For instance, the /e/ symbol does not mean that your students must produce a specific vowel quality, but rather, they must produce a vowel which is clearly different from /æ/ or /ɪ/.

4.2 Goes well with …

… PronPack 1.6, PronPack 2.3, PronPack 3.1 Version 2, and **3.3** vowel pairs for a lesson on short vowels.

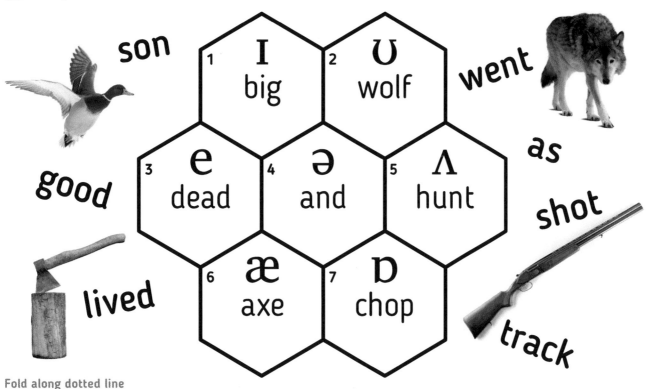

son

went

good

as

shot

lived

track

1 I big	**2** ʊ wolf	
3 e dead	**4** ə and	**5** ʌ hunt
6 æ axe	**7** ɒ chop	

Fold along dotted line

- -

Big Jack and Little Zack
Lived up in the woods
Jack was good at hunting
And Zack, at chopping wood

Jack got up
And had a cup
And went off with his gun
Had some luck
And shot a duck
And cooked it for his son

That son of Jack's
Took an axe
And went off up the track
Cut some wood
Said that's good
And put it on his back

As Zack packed
A wolf attacked
It jumped on that lad's head
That's when Jack
Ran up the track
And shot that big dog dead

Pronunciation Poems

That Girl

4.3

Background

This activity is based on a poem containing many examples of words with the vowels /eə, ɑː, ɜː, ɔː, ɪə/. These vowels usually occur before a letter *r* in the spelling.

Flexi: The letter *r* after a vowel is pronounced in some accents such as standard American English, but not in others, such as standard British English.

Presentation

Show the class some photos of young people. Ask students to describe their appearance.

Activity

1. Give out the *Worksheet 4.3*. Ask students to fold it along the dotted line and look at only the top half of the page for now. Tell them to put the words above the table into the correct column according to the vowel sound. Check vocabulary as necessary: **1** – *stare*; **2** – *arm*; **3** – *skirt*; **4** – *short*; **5** – *appears*

2. Check the answers and practise pronouncing the words.

3. Ask students to open the page out and look at the poem. Tell them to complete the poem with the words from the exercise at the top of the page.

4. Say the rhyme, **That Girl** (below, with completions), or play *Audio 4.3–1* (a spoken version of the poem) or *Audio 4.3–2* (a song version of the poem) and ask students to check their answers. Then check **answers** together as a class. Notice that in the song version of the poem, the title of the song appears as a refrain after line 4, 8 and 12.

> ### That Girl
> *That girl there with purple* **1** **hair**
> *Doesn't care if people* **2** **stare**
> *Leather jeans and sleeveless* **3** **shirt**
> *Never wears a dress or* **4** **skirt**

(That Girl...)

Nothing smart of any ⁵ **sort**
Dyes her hair and wears it ⁶ **short**
She's doing no one any ⁷ **harm**
Wearing bracelets up her ⁸ **arm**
(That Girl...)

She's not as hard as she ⁹ **appears**
With dark tattoos and pierced ¹⁰ **ears**
She likes that look, she plays that ¹¹ **part**
But that girl's got the warmest ¹² **heart**
(That Girl...)

5. Tell students to add at least one word from the poem to each column in the table. Check *answers* below.

1. eə$^{(r)}$	2. ɑː$^{(r)}$	3. ɜː$^{(r)}$	4. ɔː$^{(r)}$	5. ɪə$^{(r)}$
there	smart	girl	warm	pierced
care	dark	purple		
wear				

6. Say the poem again, or play *Audio 4.3-1* or *Audio 4.3-2* and ask students to listen and pay attention to the sound of the words with the vowel sounds in the table.

7. Say the poem again, or play *Audio 4.3-1* or *Audio 4.3-2* and ask students to sing along.

8. Ask the class to say or sing the poem together. You may use *Audio 4.3-3* (the backing track of the song) to give them the music to sing over.

4.3 Goes well with ...

... **PronPack 1.4** and **PronPack 2.2** for a lesson on r-coloured vowels.

appears   skirt   arm   stare   short

¹ eə⁽ʳ⁾	² ɑː⁽ʳ⁾	³ ɜː⁽ʳ⁾	⁴ ɔː⁽ʳ⁾	⁵ ɪə⁽ʳ⁾
hair	part heart harm	shirt	sort	ears

Fold along dotted line

- -

That girl there with purple ¹......................
Doesn't care if people ²......................
Leather jeans and sleeveless ³......................
Never wears a dress or ⁴......................

Nothing smart of any ⁵......................
Dyes her hair and wears it ⁶......................
She's doing no-one any ⁷......................
Wearing bracelets up her ⁸......................

She's not as hard as she ⁹......................
With dark tattoos and pierced ¹⁰......................
She likes that look, she plays that ¹¹......................
But that girl's got the warmest ¹²......................

Pronunciation Poems

Cat and Mouse

4.4

A cat, I [10]	I thought it thr
A cat, no [11]	Just share the
Would keep them [12]	with a cat and
A cat would scout	
And hunt about	

TEACHING FOCUS

To familiarize students with the vowels spelt with the digraph **ou**
/aʊ, uː, ɒ, ʌ, ɔː, ə/

MINIMUM LEVEL

Pre-intermediate

ACTIVITY

Chanting or reciting

WORKSHEETS

PronPack Worksheet 4.4
Print one copy for each student

AUDIO FILES

Background

This activity is based on a poem containing a large number of words with the vowel spelling **ou**. This is notoriously difficult for students because it can be pronounced as six different sounds: /aʊ, uː, ɒ, ʌ, ɔː, ə/. The poem contains examples of all of these, such as **found, group, cough, enough, four and curious**.

Activity

1. Give out the *Worksheet 4.4*. Ask students to look at the list of words in **Group A** and match them with the assorted words in **Group B** at the top of the page. Check answers and pronunciation. Check vocabulary as necessary: *house – **mouse**; cough – **off**; sound – **around**; four – **more**; through – **do**; bought – **though**t; doubt – **out**; enough – **stuff**; curious – **furious***

2. Explain that the text below **Groups A** and **B** is a poem. Point out that the last words in each pair of lines rhyme. Tell students to put the words from the matching exercise into gaps **1-8**.

3. Say the poem, **Cat and Mouse** (below, with completions), or play *Audio 4.4-1* and ask students to check their answers. Then check the **_answers_** together as a class. Check vocabulary and encourage students to guess the meaning of unknown words from context.

Cat and Mouse

I found a mouse
Was in the house
*It heard me [1] **cough**_*
*And hurried [2] **off**_*
*I heard a [3] **sound**_*
*And looked [4] **around**_*
*I found some [5] **more**_*
*A group of [6] **four**_*

*So what to [7] **do**_?*
*I thought it [8] **through**_*
*It's time I [9] **bought**_*
*A cat, I [10] **thought**_*
*A cat, no [11] **doubt**_*

*Would keep them [12] **out***
A cat would scout
And hunt about

However...

The cat I bought's
A lazy sort
*Not fast [13] **enough***
*To do that [14] **stuff***
*Won't chase a [15] **mouse***
*Around the [16] **house***
*Not even [17] **curious***
*Makes me [18] **furious**!*

What to do? I thought it through
Just share the house, with a cat and a mouse

4. Draw the table below on the board, including the phonemic symbols and one example word for each column. Tell students to copy it and add words containing **ou** from the poem in the correct column, according to the vowel sound. Check the *answers*.

1. aʊ	2. ɒ	3. ɔː	4. uː	5. ʌ	6. ə
found	cough	four	group	enough	curious
mouse		bought	through		furious
house		thought			
sound					
around					
doubt					
out					
scout					

Flexi: For an American version combine columns **2** and **3** and put the symbol /ɑ/ at the top. Renumber the remaining columns.

5. Say the poem again, or play *Audio 4.4-1*, ask students to listen and pay attention to the sound of the words with the vowel spelling **ou**.

6. Say the poem again, but leave a pause after each two lines for the students to repeat.

7. Ask the class to say the poem together in chorus.

4.4 Goes well with ...

... **PronPack 1.5**, **PronPack 2.2** Version 5 and **2.12** for a lesson on vowels spelt with two letters.

4.4 Cat and Mouse

Match the rhyming words in groups A and B. Put the words into the poem.

A.
house   four   doubt
cough   through   enough
sound   bought   curious

B.
furious   do   thought
more   stuff   around
off   mouse   out

I found a mouse
Was in the house
It heard me ¹..............
And hurried ²..............
I heard a ³..............
And looked ⁴..............
I found some ⁵..............
A group of ⁶..............

So what to ⁷..............?
I thought it ⁸..............
It's time I ⁹..............
A cat, I ¹⁰..............
A cat, no ¹¹..............
Would keep them ¹²..............
A cat would scout
And hunt about

However...

The cat I bought's
A lazy sort
Not fast ¹³..............
To do that ¹⁴..............
Won't chase a ¹⁵..............
Around the ¹⁶..............
Not even ¹⁷..............
Makes me ¹⁸.............. !

What to do?
I thought it through
Just share the house,
with a cat and a mouse!

Pronunciation Poems · Schwa Limericks

4.5

TEACHING FOCUS

To raise awareness of the sound and various spellings of the weak vowel /ə/

MINIMUM LEVEL

Pre-intermediate

ACTIVITY

Chanting or reciting

WORKSHEETS

PronPack Worksheet 1.2
Print one copy for each student

AUDIO FILES

Background

The most common sound in native accents of English is the weak vowel schwa /ə/. This sound occurs in unstressed syllables in polysyllabic words, as well as weak forms of grammatical words such as pronouns, prepositions, auxiliary verbs and articles.

Presentation

1. Write **Japan** and **Japanese** on the board, with the syllable **pan** circled. Say the two words aloud and ask students which syllable is stressed (**pan** in **Ja*pan***, **ese** in **Japan*ese***).

2. Say the words again and ask students to pay attention to the vowel sound in **pan**. Get them to notice that the vowel sound in the **pan** of **Japan** is strong, whereas in the **pan** of **Japanese** it is weak. Explain that vowel sounds are often pronounced weak in this way when a syllable is unstressed.

3. Write the symbol /ə/ on the board and explain that this sound is known as schwa. It is pronounced with the tongue and lips in a relaxed position, and is very short – so short that you can hardly hear it.

Activity

1. Give out the *Worksheet 4.5*. Explain that there are four poems (of a type known as a limerick). In every place where a vowel is pronounced as schwa, the spelling has been changed: the normal spelling has been replaced with the schwa symbol /ə/.

2. Say the poems, **Limericks 1 – 4** (below, with corrections) or play *Audio 4.5-1* (the limericks 1-4 read aloud).

3. Ask students to write the correct spellings of the vowel sounds written with a schwa symbol /ə/. Check the **answers** underlined in the full poems below. Go over vocabulary as necessary. Point out that schwa can be spelt in many different ways.

Flexi: Where there is an **r** after the schwa, it may or may not be pronounced, depending on accent. Students can choose to pronounce the **r** or not.

Limerick 1

*I met **an** **a**ccountant fr**o**m Spain*
*Whose cust**o**mers never c**o**mplain*
*She now c**a**n **a**fford*
*T**o** travel **a**broad*
***A**nd fill up h**e**r bath with Champagne*

Limerick 2

*I know **a**n old wait**e**r called Trev**o**r*
*Whose cust**o**mers wait f**o**rev**e**r*
*He lets you grow thinn**e**r*
*While waiting f**o**r dinn**e**r*
***A**nd says 'Bett**e**r late th**a**n nev**e**r!'*

Limerick 3

*I met **a** young man fr**o**m Maur**i**ti**u**s*
*Whose moth**e**r was so sup**e**rstitio**u**s*
*She said th**a**t **a** ghost*
*H**a**d eaten h**e**r toast*
***A**nd th**e** ghost said th**e** toast w**a**s delicio**u**s*

Limerick 4

***A** film crew w**a**s off t**o** Milan*
*B**u**t nothing w**a**s going t**o** plan*
*Th**e** cinem**a**togr**a**pher*
*(Not **a** great geogr**a**ph**e**r)*
*Got on **a** plane t**o** J**a**pan*

4. Say the poems aloud, pausing after each line for students to repeat. Be sure to put the stress on the bold syllables.

5. Say the poems together with the students in chorus.

6. Tell students to choose one of the poems and practise it, in preparation of performing it to the class. Then get a few volunteers to do so.

Flexi: Students do not have to produce a specific vowel quality for the sound /ə/ – it is pronounced differently by different people and in different accents. However, make sure that your students do not stress this vowel sound.

4.5 Goes well with ...

... **PronPack 1.11**, **PronPack 2.4** Version 2 and **PronPack 4.17** for a lesson on weak forms.

1. I **met** ən əc**count**ənt frəm **Spain**
   Whose **cust**əmə⁽ʳ⁾s nevə⁽ʳ⁾ cəm**plain**
   She **now** cən ə**fford**
   Tə **trav**əl ə**broad**
   ənd **fill** up hə⁽ʳ⁾ **bath** with Cham**pagne**

2. I **know** ən old **wait**ə⁽ʳ⁾ called **Trev**ə⁽ʳ⁾
   Whose **cust**əmə⁽ʳ⁾s **wait** fərevə⁽ʳ⁾
   He **lets** you grow **thin**nə⁽ʳ⁾
   While **wait**ing fər **din**nə⁽ʳ⁾
   ənd **says** 'Bettə⁽ʳ⁾ **late** thən **nev**ə⁽ʳ⁾!'

3. I **met** ə young **man** frəm Mau**rit**iəs
   Whose **moth**ə⁽ʳ⁾ was **so** supər**stit**iəs
   She **said** thət ə **ghost**
   Həd **eat**ən hə⁽ʳ⁾ **toast**
   ənd thə **ghost** said thə **toast** wəs de**lici**əs

4. ə **film** crew wəs **off** tə Mi**lan**
   Bət **noth**ing wəs **go**ing tə **plan**
   Thə **cin**əmə**tog**rəphə⁽ʳ⁾
   (**Not** ə great **geog**rəphə⁽ʳ⁾)
   Got on ə **plane** tə Jə**pan**

Hannah's Horse

4.6

TEACHING FOCUS

To familiarize students with the consonant /h/

MINIMUM LEVEL

Pre-intermediate

ACTIVITY

Chanting or reciting

WORKSHEETS

PronPack Worksheet 4.6
Print one copy for each student

AUDIO FILES

Background

This activity is based on a poem containing many examples of the sound /h/, usually at the beginning of a word. It will be especially useful for students who mispronounce this sound or drop it altogether.

Flexi: It is quite normal to drop it in pronouns such as *he* and *his*, or the auxiliary verb *have* or *has* and, many native speakers drop the *h* in other words too. However, your students would be best advised <u>not</u> to drop it except in pronouns and auxiliary verbs.

Activity

1. Give out the *Worksheet 4.6*. Explain that the text is a poem, but there was a problem with the keyboard, and it failed to insert the letter *h* in many of the words. For example, in the first line, the letter *h* is missed off the words *husband* and *horse*. Tell students to read the poem and add the missing letters.

2. Say the rhyme, **Hannah's Horse** (below, with corrections), or play *Audio 4.6-1* (a spoken version of this poem over a background beat) and ask students to check their answers. They may not be able to do this from listening alone, however, so check the answers together as a class afterwards. The missing letters are ***underlined*** below. Check vocabulary as necessary.

> Hannah's Horse
>
> *When Hannah's **h**usband bought a **h**orse*
> *Hannah didn't mind*
> *When Hannah's **h**usband ran away*
> ***H**e left **h**is **h**orse behind*
>
> *Now the **h**orse is Hannah's friend*
> *She keeps **h**im in the **h**ouse*
> *Hannah says, 'Quite **h**onestly*
> ***H**e's better than a spouse!'*
>
> *Hannah **h**ates to leave that **h**orse*
> *For more than **h**alf a day*
> *She **h**urries **h**ome with **h**appy **h**eart*
> *To feed him **h**oney and **h**ay*

How Hannah loves to ride that horse
And stroke it's hairy head
How hard it is to say goodnight
And head upstairs to bed

If Hannah's husband calls one day
Hoping for divorce
Happily she'll say 'OK'
If she can have the horse
Happily she'll say 'OK'
If she can have the horse

3. Explain that in English, the letter *h* at the start of a word is usually pronounced, except in pronouns such as *he* and *her* (see *Background section* above).

   Ask students to find one word in this poem where letter *h* at the start of a word is not pronounced (answer = *honestly*). Other words where the h is silent include *hour*, *heir* and *honour*.

4. Say the poem, pausing after every two lines to give students time to repeat. Remind them to be sure to pronounce the *h*.

5. Ask the class to say the poem together in chorus.

Flexi: The *h* is usually silent after a *w* in words like **when**. However, some speakers (from Scotland for example) do pronounce it – /hwen/.

Some words are missing the letter 'h'. Add it where necessary.

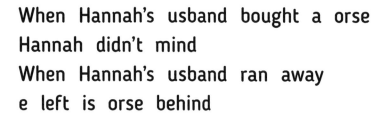

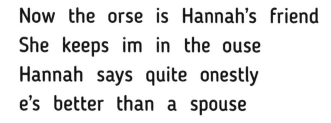

When Hannah's usband bought a orse
Hannah didn't mind
When Hannah's usband ran away
e left is orse behind

Now the orse is Hannah's friend
She keeps im in the ouse
Hannah says quite onestly
e's better than a spouse

Hannah ates to leave that orse
For more than alf a day
She urries ome with appy eart
To feed im oney and ay

ow Hannah loves to ride that orse
And stroke its airy ead
ow ard it is to say goodnight
And ead upstairs to bed

If Hannah's usband calls one day
oping for divorce
appily she'll say okay
If she can ave the orse
appily she'll say okay
If she can ave the orse

One Windy Wednesday

4.7

TEACHING FOCUS

To familiarize students with the consonant /**w**/

MINIMUM LEVEL

Pre-intermediate

ACTIVITY

Chanting or reciting

WORKSHEETS

PronPack Worksheet 4.7
Print one copy for each student

AUDIO FILES

Background

This activity is based on a poem containing many examples of the sound /w/, usually at the beginning of a word. The activity will be especially useful for students who mispronounce this sound.

Activity

1. Give out the *Worksheet 4.7*. Explain that the text is a poem, but there are typing mistakes. The last word in each line contains one wrong letter. For example, in the first line, the word **ear** should be **eat**. The correct letters are ***underlined*** below

    Tell students to read the poem and guess what the other wrong letters are.

2. Say the rhyme, **One Windy Wednesday** (below, with corrections), or play *Audio 4.7–1* (poem spoken) and ask students to check their answers. They may not be able to do this from listening alone, however, so check the answers together as a class afterwards. Ask students to guess the meaning of any new words from context.

    One Windy Wednesday
    *Wayne took Wendy out to ea**t***
    *One windy Wednesday **n**ight*
    *Wayne was in his well-worn **j**eans*
    *While Wendy wore just whi**t**e*

    *They found a place with whitewashed **w**alls*
    *Which Wendy thought was **s**weet*
    *A waiter went to welcome the**m***
    *And showed them to a **s**eat*

    *The waiter brought them **w**ater*
    *And Wendy wanted wi**n**e*
    *The waiter said, There's only w**h**ite*
    Which Wendy said was fine

    *When Wayne said, Can I ask a **q**uestion?*
    *Wendy said, Yes, **w**hat?*
    *When Wayne said, Will you marry **m**e?*
    *Wendy said, 'Why n**o**t?'*

3. Explain that in English, the sound /w/ is usually spelt with the letter *w*. Ask students to find two words in this poem where it isn't (answer = **one** /wʌn, wɒn/; **question** /ˈkwestʃən/).

4. Say the poem, pausing after every two lines to give students time to repeat. Remind them to pay attention to the sound /w/

5. Ask the class to say the poem together in chorus.

4.7 Goes well with ...

... **PronPack 2.2** Version 2 and **PronPack 3.4** Version 2 for a lesson on semi-vowels.

Find one wrong letter in the last word in each line.

Wayne took Wendy out to ear
One windy Wednesday light
Wayne was in his well-worn beans
While Wendy wore just while

They found a place with whitewashed halls
Which Wendy thought was tweet
A waiter went to welcome they
And showed them to a meat

The waiter brought them later
And Wendy wanted wife
The waiter said, There's only write
Which Wendy said was find

When Wayne said, Can I ask a guestion?
Wendy said, Yes, that?
When Wayne said, Will you marry be?
Wendy said, Why nut?

Luck

Laura ¹............ her friend's umbrella
²............ it on the train

TEACHING FOCUS

To familiarize students with the consonants /r/ and /l/

MINIMUM LEVEL

Pre-intermediate

ACTIVITY

Reciting or singing

WORKSHEETS

PronPack Worksheet 4.8
Print one copy for each student

AUDIO FILES

Background

This activity is based on a poem containing many words with the consonants /r/ and /l/. It will be especially useful for students who find either of these sounds difficult to distinguish while listening or to produce while speaking.

Activity

1. Give out the *Worksheet 4.8*. Explain that the text is a poem. Ask them read the poem and put the words above the poem into the correct gaps. Check vocabulary as necessary.

2. Say the poem **Luck** (below, with completions), or play *Audio 4.8-1* (a song of the poem, with the last verse repeated) or *Audio 4.8-2* (spoken version) and ask students to check their answers. Then check **_answers_** together.

> Luck
>
> *Laura ¹ **lost** her friend's umbrella*
> *² **Left** it on the train*
> *Feeling very ³ **sorry***
> *She ⁴ **ran** home in the rain*
>
> *Larry didn't have to ⁵ **worry***
> *When he ⁶ **felt** the rain*
> *He'd found a ⁷ **red** umbrella*
> *Lying on the ⁸ **train***
>
> *Luck is ⁹ **like** a game of chance*
> *And everyone must ¹⁰ **play***
> *Laura's piece of ¹¹ **rotten** luck*
> *Was Larry's ¹² **lucky** day*

3. Read out the poem, leaving space after every two lines for students to repeat.

4. Say the poem (above), or play *Audio 4.9-1* or *Audio 4.9-2* and ask students to say it or sing it together in chorus.

4.8 Goes well with ...

... **PronPack 3.2** Version 3, **3.5** Version 3 and **PronPack 4.8** for a lesson on *r* versus *l*.

4.8 Luck

Put the words in the poem.

Laura

like   lost   play   lucky   ran   rotten   train   worry   sorry   left   red   felt

Laura [1]............... her friend's umbrella
[2]............... it on the train
Feeling very [3]...............
She [4]............... home in the rain

Larry didn't have to [5]...............
When he [6]............... the rain
He'd found a [7]............... umbrella
Lying on the [8]...............

Luck is [9]............... a game of chance
And everyone must [10]...............
Laura's piece of [11]............... luck
Was Larry's [12]............... day

Larry

Pronunciation Poems 4.9

A Footballer's Story

eorgie sees a football **w**atch
nd thinks, "That jo**g**'s for me
hose guys **j**ust earn a fortune
nd how hard can it be?
hagine just how **s**uch they charge

TEACHING FOCUS

To familiarize students with the consonants /tʃ/ and /dʒ/

MINIMUM LEVEL

Intermediate

ACTIVITY

Chanting or reciting

WORKSHEETS

PronPack Worksheet 4.9
Print one copy for each student

AUDIO FILES

Background

This activity is based on a poem containing many examples of the sounds /tʃ/ and /dʒ/. The activity will be especially useful for students who mispronounce these sounds.

Activity

1. Give out *Worksheet 4.9*. Explain that the text is a poem, but there are typing mistakes. All of the letters in bold are wrong. For example, the *w* of *watch* in the first line should be *m* to make the word **m**atch. Ask students to read the poem and guess what the correct letters should be.

2. Say the rhyme, *A Footballer's Story* (below with corrections), or play *Audio 4.9.1* (a spoken version of this poem) and ask students to check their answers. They may not be able to do this from listening alone, however, so check the **answers** together as a class afterwards. Ask students to guess the meaning of unknown vocabulary from context and check their ideas.

A Footballer's Story

Georgie sees a football **m**atch
And thinks, 'That jo**b**'s for me
Those guys **m**ust earn a fortune
And how hard can it be?'
Imagine just how **m**uch they charge
For jogging round a p**i**tch
They only play one **m**atch a week
But man, those guys are ri**ch**!'

So Georgie **j**oins a bunch of kids
Out playing with a ball
They've made a pitch and drawn a goa**l**
With chalk **l**ines on a wall
And Georgie learns to kick the ball
And **c**atch it with his feet
Before too long, our George becomes
The best kid on the street

Then one day at Georgie's school
*They choose **h**im for the team*
And Georgie scores in every match
*He's every co**a**ch's dream*
Then one day a talent scout
Comes to watch a game
*He **w**atches Georgie on the pitch*
And asks him for his name

The rest, they say, is history
*And now our Georgie's ric**h***
He's made himself a fortune
*From running round a p**i**tch*

3. Draw and empty version of the table below on the board, and add one word for each sound as an example. Ask students to complete the table with the words in the poem which contain these sounds.

tʃ	dʒ
match fortune much pitch match rich bunch chalk catch choose coach watch	George job imagine just charge jogging joins

4. Say the poem, pausing after every two lines to give students time to repeat. Remind them to pay attention to the sounds /tʃ/ and /dʒ/.

5. Ask the class to say the poem together in chorus.

4.9 Goes well with ...

... **PronPack 1.8**, **PronPack 2.2** Version 2, **PronPack 3.3** consonant pairs, **3.4** Version 3 and **PronPack 4.10** for a lesson on fricatives and affricates.

The letters in bold are typing mistakes. Correct them.

Georgie sees a football **w**atch
And thinks, "That jo**g**'s for me
Those guys **j**ust earn a fortune
And how hard can it be?
Imagine just how **s**uch they charge
For jogging round a p**a**tch
They only play one **c**atch a week
But man, those guys are ric**e**!

So Georgie **c**oins a bunch of kids
Out playing with a ball
They've made a pitch and drawn a goa**t**
With chalk **n**ines on a wall
And Georgie learns to kick the ball
And **w**atch it with his feet
Before too long, our George becomes
The best kid on the street

Then one day at Georgie's school
They choose **J**im for the team
And Georgie scores in every **m**arch
He's every co**u**ch's dream
Then one day a talent scout
Comes to **m**atch a game
He **c**atches Georgie on the pitch
And asks him for his name

The rest, they say, is history
And now our Georgie's ric**e**
He's made himself a fortune
From running round a p**a**tch

Sue's Shoes

Sue buys shoes,
So many shoes a
It seems she can
She chooses sho
She tries on sho
She's got enough
She's short of ca
But Sue buys mo

TEACHING FOCUS

To familiarize students with the consonant minimal pair /s/ and /ʃ/

MINIMUM LEVEL

Pre-intermediate

ACTIVITY

Chanting or reciting

WORKSHEETS

PronPack Worksheet 4.10 Print one copy for each student

AUDIO FILES

Background

This activity is based on a poem containing many examples of the consonants /s/ and /ʃ/, including minimal pairs such as **same** and **shame**. The activity will be especially useful for students who have difficulty in distinguishing these sounds.

Presentation

Ask students to tell you about things they collect or buy a lot of.

Activity

1. Give out the *Worksheet 4.10*. Ask students to match the rhyming words in columns **A** and **B**. Check vocabulary as necessary: *socks* – **shocks**; *herself* – **shelf**; *same* – **shame**; *sore* – **sure**; *fasten* – **fashion**; *Sue's* – **shoes**; *sort* – **short**

2. Say random words from the exercise and ask students to say if they hear **A** or **B**. For **shelf**, say, **her shelf** so that it is a minimal pair with **herself**.

3. Tell students to do the same in pairs, taking turns to speak.

4. Tell students to complete the poem with the words from the exercise. Some words are used more than once. Ask students to guess the meaning of unknown vocabulary from context and check their ideas.

5. Say the rhyme, **Sue's Shoes** (below, with completions), or play *Audio 4.10-1* (spoken version of the poem) or *Audio 4.10-2* (a fast spoken version of this poem over a background beat) and ask students to check their answers. They may not be able to do this from listening alone, however, so check the **answers** together as a class afterwards.

Sue's Shoes

Sue's got shoes, Sue's got [1] **shoes**
A hundred shoes, and they're all [2] **Sue's**
How many shoes are on her [3] **shelf**?
She isn't even sure [4] **herself**!
Some won't fit, some won't [5] **fasten**
Some are simply out of [6] **fashion**
Lost their shine, it's such a [7] **shame**!
But Sue will keep them, all the [8] **same**

Sue's got boots of every [9] **sort**
Some are long, some are [10] **short**
Some just make her feet grow [11] **sore**
Sue should throw them out, for [12] **sure**
She's also got ten shelves of [13] **socks**
She's got so many socks, it [14] **shocks**
Some have holes, it's such a [15] **shame**!
But Sue will keep them, all the [16] **same**

Sue buys shoes, Sue buys [17] **shoes**
So many shoes, and they're all [18] **Sue's**
It seems she just can't stop [19] **herself**
She chooses shoes from every [20] **shelf**
She tries on shoes in every shop
She's got enough, but just can't stop
She's short of cash, it's such a [21] **shame**!
But Sue buys more shoes, all the [22] **same**

6. Ask students to find examples of other words in the poem containing sounds /s/ and /ʃ/, apart from the ones in the exercise.

   Here are the **answers**:

   /s/ **simply, lost, such, boots, just, so, stop**
   (note that **s** is pronounced /z/ in words like chooses and buys)

   /ʃ/ **she, shine, should, shelves, cash**

7. Say the poem, pausing after each line to give students time to repeat. Remind them to pay attention to the sounds /s/ and /ʃ/.

8. Ask the class to say the poem together in chorus.

4.10 Goes well with...

... **PronPack 1.8**, **PronPack 2.2** Version 2, **PronPack 3.3** consonant pairs, **3.4** Version 3, and **PronPack 4.9** for a lesson on fricatives and affricates.

Match the rhyming words in A and B. Use these words to complete the song.
Use some of the words more than once.

A.

socks

herself

same

sore

fasten

Sue's

sort

B.

shame

short

shelf

shoes

shocks

fashion

sure

Sue's got shoes, Sue's got [1]...................
A hundred shoes and they're all [2]...................
How many shoes are on her [3]...................?
She isn't even sure [4]...................!
Some won't fit, some won't [5]...................
Some are simply out of [6]...................
Lost their shine it's such a [7]...................
But Sue will keep them, all the [8]...................

Sue's got boots of every [9]...................
Some are long, some are [10]...................
Some just make her feet grow [11]...................
Sue should throw them out for [12]...................
She's also got ten shelves of [13]...................
She's got so many socks it [14]...................
Some have holes, it's such a [15]...................
But Sue will keep them, all the [16]...................

Sue buys shoes, Sue buys [17]...................
So many shoes and they're all [18]...................
It seems she can't stop [19]...................
She chooses shoes from every [20]...................
She tries on shoes in every shop
She's got enough but just can't stop
She's short of cash, it's such a [21]...................
But Sue buys more shoes, all the [22]...................

Flatmates

4.11

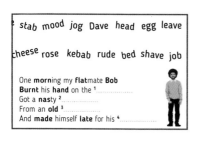

stab mood jog Dave head egg leave

cheese rose kebab rude bed shave job

One **morning** my **flatmate Bob**
Burnt his **hand** on the ¹.............................
Got a **nas**ty ².............................
From an **old** ³.............................
And **made** himself **late** for his ⁴.............................

TEACHING FOCUS

To familiarize students with voiced consonants /b, d, g, v, z/ in word-final position

MINIMUM LEVEL

Intermediate

ACTIVITY

Chanting or reciting

WORKSHEETS

PronPack Worksheet 4.11 Print one copy for each student

AUDIO FILES

Background

Voiced consonants at the end of words can be problematic for students from many different language backgrounds. Many languages do not permit voiced consonants such as /b, d, g, v, z/ at the end of a word, replacing them with unvoiced equivalents. Consequently, students may not be able to distinguish pairs of words such as **hob – hop**; **bed – bet**; **dog – dock**; **leave – leaf**; **peas – peace**.

The limericks in this activity have word-final voiced consonants at the end of every line. *Audio 4.11-1* contains the limericks read aloud.

Presentation

Write the minimal pairs **hob – hop**; **bed – bet**; **dog – dock**; **leave – leaf**; **peas – peace** on the board. Check which ones, if any, your students have problems in distinguishing. If they have difficulty, suggest the strategy of making the vowel sound shorter in the words on the right. This is because vowels are clipped before unvoiced consonants. So, for example, the **o** in **hop** sounds more clipped than the **o** in **hob**, and this helps to distinguish the **p** from the **b**.

Activity

1. Give out the *Worksheet 4.11*. Tell students to match the words in row **A** with their rhyming words in row **B**. Check vocabulary as necessary: *nose – **rose***; *hob – **job***; *sneeze – **cheese***; *stab – **kebab***; *mood – **rude***; *jog – **dog***; *Dave – **shave***; *head – **bed***; *egg – **leg***; *leave – **sleev**e*

2. Explain that the words from the rhyming exercise at the top of the page go into the gaps in the limericks below. Go through the first one **Flatmate Bob** with students as an example: **1** – *hob*, **2** – *stab*; **3** – *kebab*; **4** – *job*. Point out that **hob** and **job** rhyme with **Bob** at the end of the first line, and that **stab** rhymes with **kebab**: in a limerick, lines 1, 2 and 5 rhyme, and lines 3 and 4 rhyme.

3. Tell students to complete the rest of the limericks, using the pattern of rhymes to help them.

4. Say the rhymes **Flatmates, 1-5** (below with completions), or play *Audio 4.11-1* and ask students to check their answers. Then check **answers** together.

1. Flatmate Bob /b/

One morning my flatmate Bob
Burnt his hand on the **1 hob**
Got a nasty **2 stab**
From an old **3 kebab**
And made himself late for his **4 job**

2. Flatmate Jude /d/

One morning my flatmate Jude
Woke in a terrible **5 mood**
She hit her **6 head**
On the end of the **7 bed**
And what she said then was **8 rude**

3. Flatmate Greg /g/

One morning my flatmate Greg
Got up and fried an **9 egg**
Then went for a **10 jog**
Fell over a **11 dog**
And returned with a bite on his **12 leg**

4. Flatmate Eve /v/

One morning my flatmate Eve
Needed to hurry to **13 leave**
She ran into **14 Dave**
Who was trying to **15 shave**
And got blood all over her **16 sleeve**

5. Flatmate Louise /z/

One morning my flatmate Louise
Woke up and started to **17 sneeze**
By the time she **18 rose**
She was blowing her **19 nose**
And her face was the colour of **20 cheese**

5. Say the limericks aloud, pausing after each line for students to repeat. Be sure to put the stress on the bolded syllables.

6. Say the limericks together with the students in chorus, being careful to pronounce the voiced consonants at the end of each line.

7. Tell students to choose one of the limericks and practise it, then get a few volunteers perform them to the class.

4.11 Goes well with ...

... **PronPack 1.7**, **PronPack 3.3** consonant pairs for a lesson on stop consonants and **3.4** Version 1.

Match the rhyming words in A and B. Put the words into the poems.

A. nose hob sneeze stab mood jog Dave head egg leave

B. leg dog sleeve cheese rose kebab rude bed shave job

One **morn**ing my **flat**mate **Bob**
Burnt his **hand** on the [1]....................
Got a **nas**ty [2]....................
From an **old** [3]....................
And **made** himself **late** for his [4]....................

One **morn**ing my **flat**mate **Jude**
Woke in a **ter**rible [5]....................
She **hit** her [6]....................
On the **end** of the [7]....................
And **what** she said **then** was [8]....................

One **morn**ing my **flat**mate **Greg**
Got **up** and **fried** an [9]....................
Then **went** for a [10]....................
Fell **ov**er a [11]....................
And re**turned** with a **bite** on his [12]....................

One **morn**ing my **flat**mate **Eve**
Needed to **hur**ry to [13]....................
She **ran** into [14]....................
Who was **try**ing to [15]....................
And got **blood** all **ov**er her [16]....................

One **morn**ing my **flat**mate Lou**ise**
Woke **up** and started to [17]....................
By the **time** she [18]....................
She was **blow**ing her [19]....................
And her **face** was the **col**our of [20]....................

Kittens and Buttons

out kittens
tten by a kitten
last year
ain little kitten
in Britain
not forgotten
bit me on the ear

TEACHING FOCUS

To familiarize students with the glottal stop sound ʔ

MINIMUM LEVEL

Intermediate

ACTIVITY

Chanting or reciting

WORKSHEETS

PronPack Worksheet 4.12
Print one copy of each student

AUDIO FILES

Background

The *Kittens and Buttons* poems contain many examples of words in which the *t* is likely to be pronounced as ʔ. These are in bold text.

Flexi: The /t/ sound in English varies a lot across accents, and in different positions in a word. One very common variant which may confuse students is where the /t/ is replaced by a very short silence caused by blocking the airway in the throat. This is known as the glottal stop, or ʔ.

Activity

1. Give out *Worksheet 4.12*. Tell the students to read the poems, **Kittens and Buttons** silently and guess the meaning of new vocabulary before they hear *Audio 4.12-1* (the poems read aloud over a backing rhythm twice around). Then ask students to listen and pay special attention to how the letter *t* is pronounced where it is highlighted in bold within the two poems.

2. Ask students to say what they noticed – that the *t* was replaced by a very short silence. Explain how this silence is created by closing the throat. Tell them that they may prefer to pronounce the *t* fully in their own speech, but they should be prepared to hear the short silence when they are listening.

3. Play the *Audio 4.12-1* a few more times and let students try saying it while they listen.

4. **Optional** Write the first poem (about kittens) on the board. Ask for a volunteer to read it out. Erase a diagonal line randomly through the text. Ask for another volunteer to read out the full text applying the missing parts from memory. Gradually erase more areas of the text and repeat with more volunteers.

I know a little bit
about kittens
I got bitten by a kitten
last year
A certain little kitten
in Britain
I've not forgotten
that it bit me on the ear

I know a little bit
about buttons
I had buttons
down the front of my shirt
They fell off
when the cotton got rotten
And the buttons
got forgotten in the dirt

Steve on Skis

TEACHING FOCUS

To familiarize students with the sound of initial consonant clusters

MINIMUM LEVEL

Intermediate

ACTIVITY

Chanting or reciting

WORKSHEETS

PronPack Worksheet 4.13 Print one copy for each student

AUDIO FILES

Background

This activity is based on a poem containing many examples of consonant clusters such as /st/, /sk/, /sm/, /sk/, /str/, /sp/, /sl/, /sn/, /skr/ which usually occur at the beginning of a word. The activity will be especially useful for students who have difficulties with such clusters.

Presentation

Ask students to tell you about any sports they do, especially mountain sports or sports involving speed or risk.

Activity

1. Give out the *Worksheet 4.13*. Explain that the text is a poem, but there was a problem with the printer, and it failed to print the letter **s** in many of the words. For example, in the first line, the letter **s** is missed of the word **skate**. Tell them to read the poem and add the missing letters.

2. Say the rhyme, **Steve on Skis** (below, with corrections), or play *Audio 4.13-1* (a spoken Version of this poem over a background beat) and ask students to check their answers.

   They may not be able to do this from listening alone, however, so check answers together as a class afterwards. The missing letters are ***underlined*** in the poem below. Check vocabulary as necessary.

   Steve on Skis
   Steven Smith could never skate
   In skates he couldn't stand up straight
   'Not the sport for me,' he said
   'I think I'll learn to ski instead'
   The instructor says, 'Just take it slow
   You have to understand the snow'
   He says, 'Ok now, when you're ready'
   But Steven looks a bit unsteady

*He starts off slowly down the **s**lope*
*He's got the **s**kill to stop, we hope!*
*But soon he **s**tarts to pick up speed*
*And don't forget, he's never **s**kied!*
***S**traight ahead he sees a drop*
*But now his skis don't want to **s**top*
*Now he's **s**pinning through the air*
*And all the **s**kiers stop and stare*

*Everybody **s**tarts to scream*
*And time stands **s**till like in a dream*
Then with one almighty Whoosh!
*Steven lands **s**traight in a bush*
*Luckily it's soft and **s**trong*
*And Steve **s**teps out with nothing wrong*
*He **s**tands and waves to all the skiers*
*And **s**miles while everybody cheers*

*While Steve was falling like a **s**tone*
***S**omeone filmed it on their phone*
***U**ploaded it to internet*
*And **S**teven's now the nation's pet*

3. Draw the table below on the board, without the words in the columns. Tell students to read the poem and find examples of words to add to the columns. Do a few together as a class to give them the idea. Check answers as a class and practise the pronunciation.

/sk/	/skr/	/sl/	/sm/	/sn/	/sp/	/st/	/str/
skate	scream	slow	Smith	snow	sport	Steven	straight
ski		slowly	smiles		speed	stand	instructor
skied		slope			spinning	understand	strong
skiers						unsteady	
skill						starts	
						stop	
						stare	
						steps	
						stands	
						stone	

4. Say the poem, pausing after each line to give students time to repeat. Remind them to be careful to pronounce the consonant clusters.

5. Ask the class to say the poem together in chorus.

4.13 Goes well with ...

... **PronPack 1.9** for a lesson on consonant clusters.

There is one 's' missing in each line (except in the lines marked *). Write them in.

Steven Smith could never kate
In skates he couldn't tand up straight
'Not the port for me', he said
'I think I'll learn to ki instead'
The instructor says, 'Just take it low
You have to understand the now'
He ays, 'Okay, now when you're ready'
But teven looks a bit unsteady

He starts off slowly down the lope
He's got the kill to stop, we hope!
But soon he tarts to pick up speed
And don't forget he's never kied!
 traight ahead he sees a drop
But now his skis don't want to top
Now he's pinning through the air
And all the kiers stop and stare

Everybody tarts to scream
And time stands till like in a dream
Then with one almighty Whoosh!*
Steven lands traight in a bush
Luckily it's soft and trong
And Steve teps out with nothing wrong
He tands and waves to all the skiers
And miles while everybody cheers

While Steve was falling like a tone
 omeone filmed it on their phone
Uploaded it to internet*
And teven's now the nation's pet!

Pronunciation Poems) Lost

4.14

> You're lost
> You'll never fin
> You're lost
> And you're nev

TEACHING FOCUS

To familiarize students with the pronunciation of –ed endings and linking in connected speech

MINIMUM LEVEL

Pre-intermediate

ACTIVITY

Chanting or reciting

WORKSHEETS

PronPack Worksheet 4.14
Print one copy for each student

AUDIO FILES

Background

This activity is based on a poem containing many examples of past simple verb endings *–ed*.

Presentation

Ask students to tell you about any time when they were lost.

Activity

1. Give out the *Worksheet 4.14*. Explain that the text is a poem, but the first two verses are printed as they are pronounced, not in normal written form. Say the poem, **Lost**, twice (the way it is written on the worksheet/below) or play *Audio 4.14-1* (a chanted version of the poem over background music) and ask students to listen and read. The syllables in **bold** show where the beat falls in the rhythm.

2. Write the first line of the poem on the board, as it appears on the worksheet. Underline the two parts which are wrongly printed:

   I walk *tin* the par *kin* the middle of the night

   Explain that this is how the line is pronounced. The *–ed* of *walked* sounds like a *t*, and it joins to the following word *in* to make *tin*. The *–k* of *park* seems to join to the following word *in* to make *kin*.

3. Tell students to read the remainder of **Verses 1** and **2** and correct the other places where the words are printed incorrectly. Check *answers*. The corrections are underlined in the poem below.

   #### Lost

   *I walk**ed in** the par**k in** the middle of the night*
   *I hurr**ied in** the dark 'cause there wasn**'t any** light*
   *I stopp**ed and I** listen**ed and I** look**ed all** around*
   *I couldn't **see a** thing **and I** couldn't **hear a** sound*

   *I switch**ed on** my phone **and I** used **it** for a light*
   *I look**ed to the** left **and I** look**ed to the** right*
   *I start**ed** feeling worr**ied and** decid**ed** to go back*
   *I look**ed all** around **but I** couldn't see the track*

You're lost, you're lost
You'll never find the track
You're lost, you're lost
You're never coming back!

4. Say the first two verses of the poem, pausing after each line to give students time to repeat. Remind them to be careful to pronounce the words as they are on the worksheet. You may need to repeat the lines (or small parts of the lines) several times to give students more opportunity to practise.

5. Ask the class to say the poem together in chorus over the top of *Audio 4.14-1*.

6. Optional: Get the class to perform the song over the backing track *Audio 4.14-2* (the backing track, without the chanted words)

4.14 Goes well with ...

... **PronPack 2.2** Version 6 for a lesson on –ed endings.

I **walk** tin the **par** kin the **mid**dle of the **night**

I **hurry** din the **dark** 'cause there **was**n tenny **light**

I **stop** tan I **list**en dan die **look** tall a**round**

I **couldn**'t siya **thing** an die **couldn**'t hira **sound**

I **switch** ton my **phone** an die **use** dit for a **light**

I **look** to the **leff** tan die **lookt** other **right**

I **start**id feeling **worry** dan de**cid**id to go **back**

I **look** tall a**round** butta **couldn**'t see the **track**

You're lost, you're lost
You'll never find the track
You're lost, you're lost
And you're never coming back!

Bananas

4.15

TEACHING FOCUS

To familiarize students with the pronunciation of **-s** endings

MINIMUM LEVEL

Pre-intermediate

ACTIVITY

Chanting or reciting

WORKSHEETS

PronPack Worksheet 4.15
Print one copy for each student

AUDIO FILES

Background

This activity is based on a poem containing a lot of plural forms. The plural ending can be pronounced /z/, /s/ or /ɪz/, and the poem contains examples of all of these.

Activity

1. Give out the *Worksheet 4.15*. Explain that the text **Bananas** is a poem, but the underlined parts are printed as they are pronounced, not in normal written form. Say each verse twice (the way it is written on the worksheet – but see full print version below) or play *Audio 4.15-1* (poem read aloud as a rap over backing music) and ask students to listen and read. The syllables highlighted in **bold** on the worksheet, show the stressed syllables.

2. Write the third line of the poem on the board, as it appears on the worksheet: *But banan**a zarnt** the only fruit*, underline the part which is wrongly printed.

   Explain that this is how the line is pronounced. The plural **-s** of bananas is pronounced like a **z**, and it seems to be attached to the following *aren't*, creating an imaginary word *zarnt*.

3. Tell students to read the remainder of the poem and correct the other places where the words are printed incorrectly. Check ***answers***. The corrections are underlined in the poem below.

   Note that the word *and* is reduced in the connected speech of this poem – the **d** is cut, and the **n** sometimes changes according to the consonant sound at the beginning of the next word.

   Bananas
   A banana's full of vitamins
   That's true, that's very true
   *But banana**s aren't** the only fruit*
   *There are pear**s and** pea**ches** too*

   *You alwa**ys eat** bananas*
   It's time for something new
   *There are oran**ges**, date**s and** apricots*
   *And gra**pes and** apples too*

And don't forget the vegetables
It's good to eat a few
*Like lettu**ces**, lee**ks and** cabba**ges***
*And pe**as and** carrots too*

*They say that gree**ns are** good for you*
It's true, that's what they say
So eat your fruit and vegetables
*At least five ti**mes a** day!*

4. Draw the table below on the board, without the words. Tell students to copy it and put the plural forms into the correct columns according to the pronunciation of the plural ending. Check *answers*.

/s/	/ɪz/	/z/
apricots	peaches	bananas
grapes	oranges	pears
dates	lettuces	apples
leeks	cabbages	vegetables
carrots		peas
		greens

5. **Optional** Elicit or explain the rule shown below if students really want to know or you think it will help. (Note that many students will be able to do this intuitively, without knowing any explicit rule).

/s/	/ɪz/	/z/
for words ending with an unvoiced consonant: /p, t, k, f, θ/	for words ending with a friction consonant similar to s: /s, z, ʃ, tʃ, dʒ/	for words ending with a vowel or a voiced consonant: /b, d, g, v, ð, l, m, n, ŋ/

6. Say the poem **Bananas** and ask students to repeat each verse after you, or play *Audio 4.15-1* and ask students to check their answers. Then check the answers together as a class. Ask students to guess the meaning of new vocabulary from context.

7. Ask the class to say the poem together in chorus over the top of *Audio 4.15-1*.

8. **Optional** Get the class to perform the song over the backing track *Audio 4.15-2* (the backing track without the words).

4.15 Goes well with ...

... **PronPack 2.2** Version 2 and **PronPack 3.5** Version 2 for a lesson on /s/ versus /z/ and **-s** endings.

A ba**na**na's **full** of **vit**amins

That's **true**, that's **ve**ry **true**

But ba**na**na **zarnt** the **on**ly **fruit**

There are **pear** zum **peach** iz **too**

You **al**way **zeep** ba**na**nas

It's **time** for **some**thing **new**

There are **or**ange iz, **date** sun **ap**ricots

And **grape** sun **app**les **too**

And **don't** for**get** the **vege**tables

It's **good** to **eat** a **few**

Like **lett**uce iz, **leek** sung **cabb**age iz

An **pea** zung **carr**ots **too**

They **say** that **green** zer **good** for you

It's **true**, that's **what** they **say**

So **eat** your **fruit** and **vege**tables

At **least** five **time** ze **day**!

Further Education

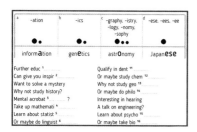

a -ation	b -ics	c -graphy, -istry, -logy, -nomy, -sophy	d -ese, -ees, -ee
•●	•●	•●●	●
inform**a**tion	gen**e**tics	astr**o**nomy	Japan**ese**

Further educ [1] _____
Can give you inspir [2] _____
Want to solve a mystery
Why not study history?
Mental acrobat [3] _____?
Take up mathemati [4] _____
Learn about statist [5] _____
Or maybe do linguist [6] _____

Qualify in dent [11] _____
Or maybe study chem [12] _____
Why not study geo [13] _____
Or maybe do philo [14] _____
Interesting in hearing
A talk on engineering?
Learn about psycho [15] _____
Or maybe take bio [16] _____

TEACHING FOCUS

To familiarize students with stress patterns in longer words and how it relates to suffixes

MINIMUM LEVEL

Intermediate

ACTIVITY

Chanting or reciting

WORKSHEETS

PronPack Worksheet 4.16
Print one copy for each student

AUDIO FILES

Background

This activity is based on a poem containing a lot of long words relating to the topic of education. These contain the suffixes *–ation*, *–ics*, *–logy*, *–nomy*, *–istry*, *–graphy*, *–sophy*, *–ese*, *–ee*, which all have an influence on where the stress falls in the word.

Activity

1. Copy the table below on the board, or give out the *Worksheet 4.16* and tell students to look at the table at the top of the page. Drill the pronunciation of the words and point out that the stress falls on the **bold** letters. Explain the stress patterns shown as -**Oo**, -**Ooo** and -**O**. These indicate that the stress falls on the syllable before the last, on the syllable two before the end, or on the last syllable for words with these suffixes.

a -ation	**b** -ics	**c** -logy, -nomy, -istry, -graphy, -sophy	**d** -ese, -ee
(-**Oo**)	(-**Oo**)	(-**Ooo**)	(-**O**)
inform**a**tion	gen**e**tics	astr**o**nomy	Japan**ese**

2. Give out the *Worksheet 4.16* (if you haven't already). Tell students to complete the words in the poem with the suffixes in the table.

3. Say the corrected poem **Further Education** (below with completions), or play *Audio 4.16-1* (the poem read aloud as a rap over backing music) and ask students to check their answers. Then check the **answers 1-16**, together as a class.

   Ask students to guess the meaning of new vocabulary from context.

4. Say the poem again, but leave a pause after each two lines for students to repeat. Tell them to pay attention to pronouncing the stress in the long words.

5. Ask the class to say the poem together in chorus.

*Further Educ**ation*** [1]
*Can give you inspir**ation*** [2]
Want to solve a mystery?
Why not study history?
*Mental acrobat**ics**?* [3]
*Take up mathemat**ics**!* [4]
*Learn about statist**ics*** [5]
*Or maybe do linguis**tics*** [6]

Knowing modern languages
Can bring you some advantages
*Ambitious employ**ees*** [7]
*Sit down and learn Chin**ese*** [8]
Do art and learn to draw
Or maybe study law
*Fancy electron**ics**?* [9]
*Or maybe econom**ics**?* [10]

*Qualify in dent**istry*** [11]
*Or maybe study chem**istry*** [12]
*Why not study geo**graphy**?* [13]
*Or maybe do philo**sophy**?* [14]
Interested in hearing
A talk on engineering?
*Learn about psycho**logy*** [15]
*Or maybe take bio**logy*** [16]

Further Education
Can give you inspiration
Fulfil an aspiration
With further education!

6. Tell students to copy the table from the top of the worksheet, with more space in the columns to add words from the poem, and any extra words they can think of. Below are some suggested *answers*.

a -ation (-Oo)	**b** -ics (-Oo)	**c** -logy, -nomy, -istry, -graphy, -sophy (-Ooo)	**d** -ese, -ee (-O)
education	acrobatics	biology	Chinese
inspiration	mathematics	economy	employees
aspiration	statistics	chemistry	**others:**
others:	linguistics	dentistry	Japanese
nation	economics	geography	Portuguese
abbreviation	electronics	philosophy	Vietnamese
circulation	**others:**	**others:**	Sudanese
pronunciation	ethics	geology	refugee
information	academics	astronomy	referee
organization	analytics	astrology	addressee
	antibiotics	zoology	
	genetics	gastronomy	
		biography	

4.16 Goes well with ...

... **PronPack 1.10**, **PronPack 2.7**, and **PronPack 3.8** for a lesson on word stress families.

4.16 Further Education

Complete the words in the poem with endings a, b, c or d below.

a -ation	b -ics	c -graphy, -istry, -logy, -nomy, -sophy	d -ese, -ees, -ee
●●	●●	●●●	●
inform**a**tion	gen**e**tics	astr**o**nomy	Japan**ese**

Further educ ¹............
Can give you inspir ²............
Want to solve a mystery
Why not study history?
Mental acrobat ³............ ?
Take up mathemati ⁴............
Learn about statist ⁵............
Or maybe do linguist ⁶............

Knowing modern languages
Can bring you some advantages
Ambitious employ ⁷............
Sit down and learn Chin ⁸............
Do art and learn to draw
Or maybe study law
Fancy electron ⁹............
Or maybe econom ¹⁰............

Qualify in dent ¹¹............
Or maybe study chem ¹²............
Why not study geo ¹³............
Or maybe do philo ¹⁴............
Interesting in hearing
A talk on engineering?
Learn about psycho ¹⁵............
Or maybe take bio ¹⁶............

Further education
Can give you inspiration
Fulfil an aspiration
With further education!

Vicky and Ricky

4.17

TEACHING FOCUS

To familiarize students with the weak forms of pronouns: *he, she, her, his, him, it, they, their, them*

MINIMUM LEVEL

Pre-intermediate

ACTIVITY

Chanting or reciting

WORKSHEETS

PronPack Worksheet 4.17
Print one copy for each student

AUDIO FILES

Background

This activity is based on a poem containing a lot of subject and object pronouns. These are usually pronounced very weakly in spoken English. They are unstressed and the vowel is often reduced to /ə/.

Flexi: If the pronoun begins with /h/, it is usually elided. If the pronoun ends with /r/, it isn't pronounced in many accents (including most accents in England and Wales).

Activity

1. Give out the *Worksheet 4.17*. Tell students to complete the words in the poem with the pronouns given. Tell students that some are used more than once. There may be more than one possibility.

2. Say the poem, **Vicky and Ricky** (below, with completions) or play *Audio 4.17-1* (poem read aloud as a rap over backing music) and ask students to check their answers. Then check **answers** together as a class. Check vocabulary as necessary.

Vicky and Ricky

He saw her
He liked **¹ her** *style*
She liked him
She gave **² him** *a smile*
He asked her **³ her** *name*
She said it was Vicky
She asked him **⁴ his** *name*
He said it was Ricky
   That's the story
   of Vicky and Ricky

He played the guitar
She said **⁵ she** *could sing*
She gave **⁶ him** *her number*
He gave her a ring
He took **⁷ his** *guitar*
He went to her flat
She gave him a drink
She showed him **⁸ her** *cat*

That's the story
of Vicky and Ricky

*She showed ⁹ **him** her music*
He played her a song
*They sang ¹⁰ **it** together*
They got it all wrong
That was the start
*Of ¹¹ **their** music careers*
*It made ¹² **them** both famous*
And lasted for years
That's the story
of Vicky and Ricky

3. Write the phrases below on the board. Explain that they are lines from the poem, written as they are pronounced. Tell students to find the lines. They are all in the first verse. Check answers and elicit orpoint out that the letters ***h*** and ***r*** may be cut from the pronunciation of the pronouns. Also, it may sound as if the last consonant of the verb is attached to the pronoun which follows, as in ***like tim = liked him***.

   1. E sore a

   2. She like tim

   3. She gay vim a smile

   4. E ask tara name

   5. She ask timis name

   Answers:

   1 = *He saw her;* **2** = *She liked him;* **3** = *She gave him a smile;* **4** = *He asked her her name;* **5** = *She asked him his name*

4. Say the poem again, but leave a pause after each line for students to repeat. Tell them to pay attention to the way the pronouns are reduced.

5. Ask the class to say the poem together in chorus.

6. Optional: Play the backing track *Audio 4.17-2* and tell students to chant the poem over it.

4.17 Goes well with ...

... **PronPack 1.11**, **2.4** Version 2 and **PronPack 4.5** for a lesson on weak forms.

Complete the poem with the pronouns.

their

his

she

it

them

her

him

He saw her
He liked ¹............ style
She liked him
She gave ²............ a smile
He asked her ³............ name
She said it was Vicky
She asked him ⁴............ name
He said it was Ricky
> **That's the story of
> Vicky and Ricky**

He played the guitar
She said ⁵............ could sing
She gave ⁶............ her number
He gave her a ring
He took ⁷............ guitar
He went to her flat
She gave him a drink
She showed him ⁸............ cat
> **That's the story of
> Vicky and Ricky**

She showed ⁹............ her music
He played her a song
They sang ¹⁰............ together
They got it all wrong
That was the start
Of ¹¹............ music careers
It made ¹²............ both famous
And lasted for years
> **That's the story of
> Vicky and Ricky**

Pronunciation Poems 4.18

Nobody Does it Better

TEACHING FOCUS

To familiarize students with rhythm and weak forms

MINIMUM LEVEL

Pre-intermediate

ACTIVITY

Chanting or reciting

WORKSHEETS

PronPack Worksheet 4.18
Print one copy for each student

AUDIO FILES

Background

English is characterized by a rhythm which results from patterns of stressed and unstressed words in speech.

Content words such as nouns, adjectives, adverbs and main verbs are stressed (or more accurately, the main syllable of the content word is stressed – the other syllables are unstressed).

Function words such as pronouns, articles, prepositions and auxiliary verbs are usually unstressed (but note that auxiliary verbs are stressed in contractions with **not**, because **not** is a content word).

The limericks in this activity are laid out on the page to make the rhythm visually obvious, with the stressed words falling in the same vertical line, printed in bold. The unstressed syllables are printed in a smaller size in between these beats. The **X** represents a silent beat.

Activity

1. Give out the *Worksheet 4.18*. Tell students that they are going to hear four short limericks. Ask them to listen and pay special attention to how the beat of the poems is shown on the page. Say all four **Limericks** or play *Audio 4.18-1* (poems read aloud over a chorus singing **1, 2, 3, 4**). Check vocabulary as necessary.

   Limerick 1
   There wasn't a woman in Wales
   Whose fingers were stronger than Gail's
   She could solo on drums
   With only her thumbs
   And open a tin with her nails

   Limerick 2
   There wasn't a kid in Madrid
   Who could clap his hands faster than Sid
   His hands were so quick
   It looked like a trick
   And no one could see what they did

Limerick 3

There isn't a woman in Delhi
Who likes her food hotter than Kelly
She covers her rice
With pepper and spice
And likes how it burns in her belly

Limerick 4

There isn't a girl in Berlin
Who's faster on wheels than Lynne
She cycles her bike
As fast as you like
And gets there before you begin

2. Ask students to say which kinds of words are **stressed** (larger print on the student's worksheet) and which are **unstressed** (smaller print). Elicit that verbs, nouns, adjectives and negatives are stressed, while articles, pronouns, prepositions and auxiliary verbs are unstressed.

3. Play the audio a few more times and let students try saying it while they listen.

4. Get students to choose their favourite of the four limericks and practise saying it. Then get them to say their limerick out loud while the rest of the class chant the numbers **1-2-3-4** to set the rhythm.

   Alternatively, half the class could be saying the limerick while the other half chant the numbers.

4.18 Goes well with ...

... **PronPack 1.12** for a lesson on rhythm.

1.	2.	3.	4.
There **was**n't a	**wom**an in	**Wales**	x
Whose **fing**ers were	**strong**er than	**Gail's**	x
She could **sol**o on	**drums** with	**on**ly her	**thumbs**
And **op**en a	**tin** with her	**nails**	x

There **was**n't a	**kid** in Ma	**drid**	x
Who could **clap** his hands	**fast**er than	**Sid**	x
His **hands** were so	**quick** it	**looked** like a	**trick**
And **no** one could	**see** what they	**did**	x

There **is**n't a	**wom**an in	**Del**hi	x
Who **likes** her food	**hott**er than	**Kell**y	x
She **cov**ers her	**rice** with	**pepp**er and	**spice**
And **likes** how it	**burns** in her	**bell**y	x

There **is**n't a	**girl**in Ber	**lin**	x
Who's **fas**ter on	**wheels** than	**Lynne**	x
she **cy**cles her	**bike** as	**fast** as you	**like**
And **gets** there	be**fore** you	be**gin**	x

About the Author

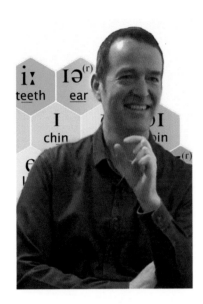

Mark Hancock started teaching English over 30 years ago and wrote his first English language teaching book – *Pronunciation Games* – over 20 years ago. His approach in both teaching and writing ELT materials is to engage the learner and inspire their intrinsic interest in the content and in the process of the lesson. This is driven by his belief that teaching and learning a language can and should be an enjoyable experience.

He studied Geography and Philosophy at St. Andrews University, followed by teacher training courses and finally an MA in Teaching English from Aston University. Mark has taught in Sudan, Turkey, Brazil, Spain and currently lives and works in the UK. Apart from teaching and writing, he also presents at international conferences and leads on short teacher training courses.

In his free time, Mark plays the saxophone and guitar, paints in oils and walks in the mountains.

By the same author

ELT Pronunciation and Skills

- *Pronunciation Games* (CUP 1995)
- *English Pronunciation in Use Intermediate* (CUP 2003, 2012)
- *Authentic Listening Resource Pack* (Delta 2014 – co-authored with Annie McDonald)
- *Pen Pictures 1, 2 & 3* (OUP 1999 – 2000 – co-authored with Annie McDonald)
- *Oxford Advanced Learner's Dictionary 9th Ed 'Speaking Tutor' section* (OUP 2015)
- *Empower C1 'Everyday English' sections* (CUP 2016)
- *Singing Grammar* (CUP 1999)

ELT Course Book Series

- *English Result* (OUP 2007 – 2010 – co-authored with Annie McDonald)
- *Out and About* (CUP 2015 – co-authored with Annie McDonald)
- *Winners* (OUP 2010 – co-authored with Cathy Lawday)
- *New Ways to Go* (CUP 2002 – co-authored with Penny Ur and Ramon Ribé)

Acknowledgements

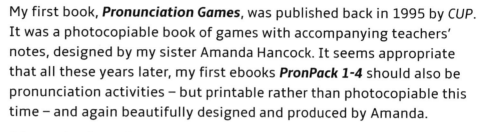

My first book, **Pronunciation Games**, was published back in 1995 by *CUP*. It was a photocopiable book of games with accompanying teachers' notes, designed by my sister Amanda Hancock. It seems appropriate that all these years later, my first ebooks **PronPack 1-4** should also be pronunciation activities – but printable rather than photocopiable this time – and again beautifully designed and produced by Amanda.

A huge thank you is also due to Annie McDonald for her editorial work and tireless encouragement, and to Henry Wong of Heliographic for his graphic design input.

I would also like to thank my students at *English in Chester* (www. english-in-chester.co.uk), who were the first to try out the activities in this book, and colleagues at that school who also trialled the material, especially Patsy Tyrer.

Last but not least I would like to thank my team of consultants/ reviewers around the globe, including:

Freya Barua *(India)*
Marina Cantarutti *(Argentina)*
Ariel Donnell-Clark *(UK)*
Cristina Gómez Martínez *(Spain)*
Ewa Grzelak *(Poland)*
Louise Guyett de Orozco *(Ireland)*
Oksana Hera *(Ukraine)*
Stella Maris Palavecino *(Argentina)*
José Mompean *(Spain)*
Lalitha Murthy *(India)*
Catarina Pontes *(Brazil)*
Jane Neill *(UK)*
Adam Scott *(UK)*
Elena Velikaya *(Russia)*

Editor: Annie McDonald
Book design: Amanda Hancock
Graphics: Heliographic
Illustration: Mark Hancock
Images: Shutterstock.com
Audio: Mark Hancock with Annie McDonald

For more information visit www.pronpack.com

Printed in Great Britain
by Amazon